FAIR DINKUM BUSINESS

Applying Traditional Aussie Values for Success in Startups and Global Business

Written & Illustrated by
WAYNE MORRIS

First Edition – September 2019

ISBN-13: 978-0-578-57443-1

This book is dedicated to:
My wonderful wife who has been my partner and
primary support for many years.

My two children of whom I am very proud and who are now
strong, contributing adults, each serving in their own way
with far more noble professions than I've had.

To my colleagues, mentors and workmates across multiple
companies in the USA and Australia – I've learnt so much from
each of you and truly appreciate the experience of getting to
know you and growing as people and professionals together.

Table of Contents

Introduction

A word about the book title – "Fair dinkum" is
Australian slang meaning true, genuine, honest.

After a long career in information technology in both Australia and USA, I started looking forward to slowing down (just a little!) and as is natural in this type of situation, began to reflect on my experiences. One part of this process was to write this book (which I've tried to keep succinct) to capture my thinking and hopefully help others who are earlier in their career journey.

I was raised in a traditional single income working family in North Queensland, Australia. My father was a fireman, a mechanic and a tractor salesman. My mother was the home maker and volunteered at my school, the local library and various community organizations. As children, we were taught the necessity and rewards of hard work, mutual respect and community values. These lessons typically came with a story that had a traditional Australian flavor.

As I made my way through the business world, I carried these values and tried to live up to them as best I could (although I acknowledge somewhat imperfectly at times). This book attempts to capture some of the more memorable and relevant Australian sayings that have been the basis of my approach to conducting myself and operating a commercial enterprise.

I've been fortunate to be able to work in a wide variety of roles, disciplines, organizations and locations. These include coding customs and border control systems for the Australian Government as a public servant, consulting and selling computing systems, managing large teams of technical professionals, product marketing, corporate marketing, business unit management, company officer and senior executive in multiple industry-leading companies, CEO and board director of a public company and senior executive of multiple startup companies. During this time, I lived and worked in ten different cities in seven states on two continents.

In my career, I've designed and introduced multiple new products, built new businesses from scratch, and formed and grew multiple high-performance teams. I've also worked without pay for many months, was nearly bankrupt once (maybe twice), and made multiple millions of dollars from my executive roles at large companies and through startup success. Throughout it all, what I'm most proud of and what brought most joy has been the relationships, mentoring and friendships I've experienced and the number of people who have wanted to do business or work with me multiple times.

As you read this book, I hope you take away some common-sense principles that you can reflect on and perhaps utilize in your own approach to business and work relationships. You might also compare the sayings I've used here with the lessons you've had both prior to and during your career.

I'd enjoy hearing about your own experiences and thoughts! To continue the conversation, follow and contribute on Twitter at @FairDinkumBiz or email me at wayne@fairdinkum.biz.

Chapter One

'Have a Captain Cook'

'Have a Captain Cook' is rhyming slang for 'have a look'. Captain James Cook was a famous explorer in the Royal Navy who, among other achievements, led the first recorded European contact with the eastern coastline of Australia.

The starting point for any product, business or team is undertaking the required research to understand aspects such as the market dynamics, customer needs, team requirements and people skills. This process can be very energizing and rewarding.

It's best to adopt a straight-forward approach to research and be prepared to modify your approach and conclusions as you go:

- Start with background investigation of broad themes and trends that might apply to your situation;
- Formulate a hypothesis of a potential outcome or result from applying specific trends;

- Develop open-ended questions that might solicit additional direct insight from the most-relevant target audience and determine appropriate incentives to obtain cooperation;
- Determine relevant sources of quantitative data and statistics that might either support or refute the hypothesis and potentially size the opportunity.

My earliest experience in this approach was not long after I moved from Australia to Silicon Valley and joined HP (or Hewlett Packard as it was known at the time). I had been in role as a product manager for a few months and it was clear that the software business unit needed another product if it was to be a successful and profitable entity within HP. Over the year-end holiday break, I spent multiple days reviewing the market dynamics to see where there might be potential opportunities, rather than enjoying holiday down time, much to my family's chagrin.

This was an interesting time for the computer industry as many companies moved from having a single, central mainframe to distributing multiple smaller computer servers closer to their business units in order to improve flexibility and timeliness of the computing services they provided. While this indeed provided greater agility and a broader range of services, it also came with larger management overhead to keep all those servers operating efficiently.

Whenever faced with a new problem such as this, it can be instructive to look at analogous issues in other industries. In this case, it occurred to me that the manufacturing industry had a similar issue with the machinery involved in complex manufacturing processes. In their case they used control systems with specialized monitors that provided alerts whenever a specific machine was experiencing a failure or sub-optimal operations.

This enabled a "management by exception" approach which allowed a single operator to monitor and control many machines.

Relating the "management by exception" approach to distributed computer servers was novel at the time. But before funding for such a product would be approved, management would need to be convinced of the opportunity and the product potential. What I needed to do was to outline the market dynamic that created the opportunity, identify the customer need and attempt to quantify both the business potential and product fit. This required a combination of primary and secondary research using available market data to show the magnitude of the move to distributed computing, as well as direct surveys to capture solution requirements, validate the product approach and assess the willingness of prospective customers to pay.

Once the data was collated, writing the report required an amount of time to ensure it was compelling, easy to understand, and utilized graphics to present information concisely with a clear summary and action plan. This was successful, funding was secured, and the product was released as HP PerfView.

Another great learning opportunity for me was when I was Director of Corporate Strategy at BMC Software. We had determined that strategically we needed to rapidly expand our product portfolio and customer base, which resulted in a project to determine acquisition candidates. I headed this effort internally and worked closely with a team from Bain & Company which was led by Dianne Ledingham. They did a very thorough job of determining our market position, segmenting the market, calculating best demonstrated penetration for each product within each segment, and hence extrapolating our maximum realistic market potential.

Then followed an exercise to identify product adjacencies and again estimate the impact by looking at the potential for the combined products across the combined customer bases. This resulted in several strategic acquisitions which significantly boosted our current revenue as well as future potential. I found the approach very enlightening and I used a similar approach in later roles to determine potential market opportunity.

In addition to research, another way to determine what customers really need is to deliver customized solutions to a problem, look for repetition and commonalities across these solutions, and to then package these as a product. This was one of the highlights of my time as CEO of Citect Corp, an Australian industrial control software company which had operations worldwide. In addition to packaged software for HMI (Human Machine Interface) and SCADA (Supervisory Control and Data Acquisition) we had a large consulting team delivering solutions to manufacturing problems such as job scheduling, optimizing operations across all the machinery in an assembly line (OEE – Overall Equipment Effectiveness) and tracking batch processes, which is very necessary if a product recall is required, particularly in the food industry.

It seemed that in many cases, the consulting contract was a repeat of work that had been performed for another customer and so we looked for common components that could be coded and packaged as a new business line, which resulted in Citect Ampla, a new family of offerings to address the nascent MES (Manufacturing Execution Systems) market.

I was fortunate in finding the right leader for this effort, Peter Long, who headed our consulting operations but also understood the business value of packaging solutions that leveraged captured intellectual property rather than simply selling "time and materials" consulting. Peter and I would collaborate again later in my career when together we founded myDIALS, which developed business intelligence software.

Sometimes market research highlights an amazing new area of opportunity that you've either been completely unaware of or simply overlooked. After Citect (which was later acquired by Schneider Electric) I returned to the USA. It was when I was looking for my next opportunity that I had one of those moments when you have to ask yourself, "where have I been that I've totally missed this?".

I went to a computing conference in Silicon Valley and was absolutely amazed by the energy and potential applications surrounding cloud computing. This was early days – Amazon had yet to start AWS (Amazon Web Services) – but Salesforce had been selling cloud-based software for a few years and the interest from the venture capital community was intense.

I felt compelled to dive right in and better understand the cloud landscape as well identify potential business applications that it could unlock, particularly in the world of business software. This led to the collaboration with Peter Long that I mentioned above to develop myDIALS as a business intelligence software offering delivered through the cloud using the software-as-a-service model.

This was a very exciting and rewarding period in my career, but I still recall being somewhat embarrassed and feeling like I'd been living in a cave when I first saw the excitement and possibility of cloud computing – and equally appreciative that it didn't totally pass me by.

Have a Captain Cook

- **Look for fundamental shifts in market dynamics and technology.**

- **Utilize primary and secondary research.**

- **Experiment with custom solutions or consulting that can be packaged into repeatable product offerings.**

Chapter Two

'Have a Go Ya Mug'

'Have a go ya mug' is a popular expression at Australian cricket matches to encourage a player to do something, to take a chance and take action.

It's one thing to do the necessary research to identify potential market and product opportunities and even to validate the product market fit through primary and secondary research and experimentation, and a very different thing to maximize the business potential.

Typically, this requires the ability to operate in uncertainty and ambiguity, without full information or data. At the core, it requires a willingness to take calculated risks and I believe this one characteristic contributes greatly to personal and professional success.

Evaluating risk/reward requires a realistic assessment of the situation and potential outcomes:

- Think through your risk tolerance based on your personal, family and financial situation – is there something that absolutely prevents you taking a risk?
- Ask "what's the worst outcome that might happen if I proceed on this path?"
- Identify the best possible outcome as well as the most likely outcome;
- Attach your best estimate of percentage probabilities to the worst, most likely and best outcomes;
- Based on likelihood of the potential outcomes and associated results, ask if the risk is worthwhile.

Throughout my career, I've been willing to take risks sometimes causing concern within my family. When I first moved to the USA it was to pursue adventure and broader business opportunities. Well maybe not entirely. I was really pursuing the woman who would become my wife and love of my life for more than 30 years (and counting). Even so, it was somewhat disconcerting that I was leaving a very good position as a leader in sales in Australia, to move to a new country with no job and in fact no legal ability to work.

However, the breadth of opportunity, particularly in Silicon Valley in the late eighty's, was staggering compared to the opportunities within the technology industry in Australia.

I was very fortunate to be selected for a product marketing/manager role within Hewlett Packard at a time when the "HP Way" was very meaningful and I relished the opportunity to learn product marketing. After being promoted to lead the marketing team and then to Business Unit Manager for system performance management software, I also had a great opportunity to learn more about being an effective manager. I certainly enjoyed my time at HP and learnt a lot as we successfully established the business into a profitable, high-growth entity within HP. However, there came a time when I had to make the next decision that involved risk.

Like many people who are on a successful trajectory within a large organization, I began to contemplate if this was to be my long-term career. After five years of growth in role and responsibility it would have been quite easy and probably rewarding to continue to climb the corporate ladder within HP.

However, it seemed that maybe there were other opportunities to make a bigger impact, most likely in a smaller organization. Coincidently, I was approached by a startup to join their executive team as Chief Marketing Officer (CMO). This meant moving to Los Angeles from Sacramento and while the company was very well funded with strong Venture Firm backing, any startup involves a degree of risk.

In this case, the risk was greater than I had anticipated, as the company was sued for trade secret violation a couple of months after I joined. While the executive team and the Board believed the suit was without merit, I learnt a lot more about the US legal system than I ever wanted to know, particularly how a larger company with deep pockets and what seemed to be a personal vendetta, could make life very difficult for a startup company and its officers. We struggled through court depositions while continuing to build out product and sell to new customers, but our funding was running low, resulting in the executive team not being paid for several months.

This was quite painful, particularly with a young family, and in the end, we put the company in Chapter 7 bankruptcy and walked away (after having one last party together – or maybe it was a wake). Two of my colleagues went into personal bankruptcy, and while I didn't have to go quite that far, it did take me a few years to recover financially and personally from this experience.

After that startup experience, you might think I'd be finished with startups, but this wasn't to be the case. After recovering to be an executive and company officer in two large public companies, and the CEO of an Australian public company, I again found myself toying with another startup.

In this case it was probably the biggest risk of all, which is when you decide along with other founders to start a new company from scratch – all while sitting around the proverbial dining table. As I found out, starting a technology company is not for the faint of heart, as there are legal costs to setup the company and upfront development work required to build the initial "minimum viable product" that must be funded before any paying customers can help offset the costs.

In addition, if you want to make early customers successful and grow quickly to maximize the market opportunity, there are rapidly escalating costs to build out the sales, support, and consulting teams. Before we could get external funding, we had to prove product market fit and our business model, particularly as we very early to market with a cloud-based "Software as a Service" offering.

This meant we had to provide initial funding through a combination of paid consulting work and my personal investments which greatly increased the risk. Even as we raised additional funding, I felt compelled to continue to invest alongside the external investors in every round of funding so that I could both influence them and have credibility given I was willing to invest on exactly the same terms as them.

This startup was much more rewarding than my first startup experience, although it also wasn't a straight line to the end result, and I'll provide more details in other chapters.

Have a Go Ya mug!

- Taking appropriate risks can lead to rewards but ensure you've calculated and are satisfied with the risk/reward potential.

- Asking "what's the worst that can happen" can help identify the fallback or worst-case scenario.

- Once you've decided to take the risk, leap at it and don't seconde-guess, as this will only cause confusion.

Chapter Three

'Go Big or Go Home'

*'Go Big or Go Home' is a saying to encourage
someone to be ambitious – to do something to
the fullest. The origin is unclear as I've heard it
in Australia, South Africa and UK long before it
was in a movie and subsequently a pop song.*

Once you've identified a potential opportunity and decided to
address it, the next question is how far do you want to take it?
While I understand small and family businesses being content
with modest growth to support a lifestyle, in the commercial
world, I've only ever been involved with organizations that wanted
to make as large an impact as possible (my time in Government
organizations was completely different!).

Every technology startup, particularly once external investors are involved, has huge ambitions to conquer their market
space and potentially impact an industry. That has certainly been
the case with the three startups I've been involved with, and

this typically involves innovation both on product development and delivery, but also with driving the go-to-market to achieve maximum scale. Of course, every startup thinks of product innovation, but I believe optimizing the go-to-market model is equally important, and not enough startups pursue a multi-channel strategy to achieve scale affordably.

At myDIALS, while we successfully sold early customers using a direct sales approach, which I believe is vital to proving product/market fit, we augmented this approach by forming a resale agreement with NetSuite which was a much larger public company, as well as an OEM agreement with Adaptive Planning which was a larger private company. Over time as we gained traction through these channels, we prioritized them and defocused away from direct sales. I believe this approach of utilizing larger channel partners is very important for enterprise class sales. This was true for myDIALS and even more important at Skytap, the last startup where I was an executive.

At Skytap, we were working with large enterprise companies to move their most critical business applications to the cloud – many of these applications had been developed over many years (maybe even multiple decades) and the underlying technology was not suited for cloud deployment. Skytap had unique and patented technology to enable the migration of these applications to the cloud with only minimal changes, resulting in significant savings and enabling these organizations to bring new innovations to the applications much more rapidly. Even though the Skytap product innovation was unique, it wasn't enough to ensure success.

Because these large companies absolutely depended on these business applications, it was difficult to convince them to trust that Skytap, a relatively small and unknown private company, would successfully support them. This meant we had to find appropriate channel partners that would bring the necessary brand recognition, credibility and support services to convince the target companies to buy the solution.

This started with an OEM agreement with IBM, which had relationships with the large enterprises we were targeting and the credibility to ensure success. Once IBM was on board, we needed other channel partners including Microsoft and large systems integrators and services companies such as Accenture. Given this priority, we evolved our go-to-market model away from direct sales and moved to a completely channel-centric model.

Continuing with the theme of evolving the business model, sometimes the opposite go-to-market model becomes necessary as the company grows and needs to take more control of product distribution.

This was the case for me when I was hired to be the CEO of Citect Corp, an Australian industrial automation software vendor. Citect had been very successful in Australia with a large market share driven by a direct sales model augmented by a network of channel partners. Outside Australia, while Citect was marketed in the USA, Europe, South Africa and Asia, it had very small market share and the typical model apart from the USA was a single exclusive distribution partner in each country.

This was problematic as Citect was becoming better known but was competing with much larger companies such as Schneider Electric, Siemens and Rockwell, and the organizations we were selling to (both commercial and Government entities) preferred to do business directly with the supplying vendor rather than with a partner. This first became apparent in South Africa where a large mining company had selected Citect as the best technology for multiple large projects worth $ multiple millions but would not place the order unless Citect was the direct contracting entity. This led to an interesting deal whereby we acquired our channel partner in South Africa in parallel with securing the first mining company order.

We followed this acquisition with similar acquisitions of the distribution partners in UK, Germany and France. In the USA, Citect already had an operating subsidiary but all sales were through a large channel network comprised primarily of very small companies that were mostly focused on consulting projects.

In this case we again took more direct control, rationalized the channel to a smaller number of more capable partners and sold the most strategic deals directly, supported by Citect's own services organization. In this case, strengthening the direct go-to-market was important and reflective of Citect's evolving market position and the related market opportunity. It became even more important as we added new higher-end offerings that were more strategic and expensive, and hence required a deeper relationship between vendor and customer.

There are also situations where only a combination of product innovation, aligned go-to-market model and an enabling business model can accelerate growth. This was the case at BMC Software.

I joined BMC to drive the marketing for PATROL, which was their first non-mainframe offering. Interestingly, BMC had acquired PATROL Software, which was a small Australian company a year earlier. It was designed to manage distributed networks of computer servers with a unique model of Agents (small units of software that would be installed on each of the computer servers) and Knowledge Modules, which held the instructions for how the Agent should behave, what metrics should be monitored, what alerts or exception conditions it should detect, and what actions it should take for each alert situation.

This was a great product innovation but had not been fully exploited at that time as it only focused on the operating system.

The flexibility of the platform meant it could be used much more broadly to support all the software layers required to support business processes including databases, middleware and applications, in addition to the underlying operating system.

However, in order to achieve this, we needed to bring together the experts in each of these various technologies (and there are many different databases, applications etc from many vendors), and provide appropriate incentives to reward them for coding the various Knowledge Models we required to cover the target market opportunity.

We achieved this with three parallel initiatives:

1. Where we could form the right partnership with the software vendor, we would work directly with them to jointly develop the Knowledge Module which would then be offered by both parties.
2. Where we couldn't form the direct partnership, we would identify an appropriate third party to develop the Knowledge Module, which we would then market and provide a royalty payment back to the partner.
3. To build awareness and momentum we developed a "Managed by PATROL" marketing program which we promoted heavily (in conjunction with partners wherever possible).

This was very successful with a rapidly expanded range of software being managed by PATROL and the "PATROL Mark" being used by many supplying vendors. Given we had modeled this somewhat on the earlier "Intel Inside" program, one highlight for me was when we reached an agreement with Intel to modify the PATROL Agent to run on the Intel chip so it could monitor the firmware.

Go Big or
Go Home!

- ■ Outsized rewards typically go to the largest players in a market or the companies with the greatest market momentum.

- ■ Achieving market share growth typically takes a combination of product innovation, the right go-to-market model and an enabling business model.

- ■ There is no correct single answer to an appropriate go-to-market model as it is dependent on the target market, customer desires and specific company situation.

Chapter Four

———

Don't Hire Drongos, Galahs or A Bull in the China Shop

'Drongo' is a mild form of insult meaning idiot or stupid person. This comes from an Australian racehorse of the same name in the 1920s that never won despite many places. 'Galah' is also used to describe a fool and is named after a noisy pink and grey cockatoo. 'Bull in the China Shop' refers to a person who is careless in the way they behave, which causes great consternation.

In any organization, but particularly in startups, hiring the right people at the right time is probably <u>the</u> key element that determines success, mediocrity or outright failure. It's not always easy to identify the best candidate, and I know throughout my career I've made some bad decisions, mostly because I didn't listen to my "gut", or I moved too quickly to hire as a matter of expediency. In every case I've come to regret the decision and have subsequently had to correct the situation by removing the person or moving them to a new role.

Whenever a hiring decision is to be made there are some clear guidelines that can help:

- Ensure you spend enough time with the person to observe them in a variety of situations – sometimes the most telling behavior is outside the formal interview process;
- Involve a representative sample of all the people who will interact with or depend on the new hire – this will also provide multiple perspectives;
- Do the appropriate amount of reference checking including "back-door" and informal checks as available and appropriate;
- Once the hiring decision is made, determine what you are prepared to offer and when you will walk away (very similar to any other negotiation);
- If after the hire you determine that something is amiss, quickly address this directly with the individual and either work towards a satisfactory resolution or remove the person from the role (either to a better suited position or entirely);
- You will hear the saying "hire slow, fire fast", but I believe more appropriate is "hire carefully, resolve issues quickly".

In many cases when taking a new managerial position, you will inherit people that will turn out to be suboptimal in their roles. In other cases, you are not the direct hiring manager, but the new hire will be part of your broader team – this is especially difficult if you have misgivings, but don't want to usurp or diminish the authority and responsibility of the hiring manager.

I've found that bad people issues typically fall into one of three categories:

- The person who is just not competent or capable in their role and not willing or able to gain the necessary skills (this is the 'drongo' category)
- The person who thinks they're very competent and struts around in a pretentious way while not being capable in their role and even worse, probably demoralizing those around them (I liken this person to the galah that looks pretty, squawks a lot, doesn't add any value and causes damage to crops).
- The person that is toxic in the organization – this could be because they are a bully, hyper-aggressive, gossips or generally causes mayhem (this is the proverbial bull in the china shop).

I've had experiences with all the above. In the drongo category, you will find people who just don't seem to understand the context of their role or the desired outcome and value they should deliver.

One person who was meant to execute marketing programs in conjunction with channel partners couldn't successfully negotiate the goals, target audience, marketing campaign tactics or the assets to be used in those campaigns with the partners. This led to dissatisfaction and confusion in both the partner organizations and in the broader marketing department and resulted in additional work, cost and wasted resources while missing the opportunity to get maximum traction in the marketplace.

Sometimes the person has ability but fails to deliver because they don't understand the true objective of their role. I've seen this happen multiple times with people who are managing data around business processes. They see their role as simply gathering and collating data and will produce wonderfully detailed reports and graphs to encapsulate the data they've collected. They fail in their role because they don't appreciate that it's not really about the data, but the insights that can be gleaned to make better decisions or optimize the processes they're managing.

My observation is that this stems not entirely from incompetence, but rather a misalignment of expectations or perhaps a lack of aptitude towards the process of discovery and analytics required to derive true insights.

The galah category seems to be most prevalent in the sales department, which is probably to be expected. I've been a salesperson in my career so hopefully I was different, but many salespeople are very good at giving the appearance of confidence and competence, where in reality they are primarily mimicking behavior they believe will appear successful, while trying to build personal relationships that might lead to some orders, and relying heavily on competent people around them.

You might argue that this is their role and to some extent it is, however the very best salespeople have both the charisma to form appropriate relationships and enough understanding and competence to add value to the customer relationships and transactions they drive.

In the first startup, I saw this firsthand with a salesperson who was more adept at manipulating management and obtaining additional draws (advances against future commissions) than in working with prospective customers to identify opportunity areas and correctly presenting and aligning an offering to deliver value. In another company, we had an individual salesperson who spent a lot of time traveling to various cities, entertaining prospects with expensive dinners and wine, but never really identifying true opportunities where we could add value and certainly not closing any deals of significance.

The "bull in a china shop" can be very dangerous. In a number of these cases, the person is competent and can add value if measured solely on their personal contributions. However, the impact on the people around them and the organization is so negative that they need to be addressed and the situation resolved no matter how much they achieve. This can be difficult as there is inertia and fear of missing their personal contribution to overcome, but I firmly believe that one toxic person can quickly spread discontent and poor behavior throughout an organization.

This person must be dealt with quickly, both to correct the specific situation and to send a message within the organization regarding personal behavior that is acceptable and valued. I've seen this mostly where a person is brought in from outside the organization to take on a new mission or to revive the organization – sometimes referred to as a "change agent". In many cases there will be some short-term benefits and performance improvement, but this will rapidly deteriorate as the effects of this type of personality becomes apparent.

The absolute worst situation you can find yourself in is when a drongo, galah or bull in a china shop becomes your manager. I've also suffered through this situation and have determined that the best outcome is simply to move on. You won't be able to change them or their behavior, and while you could decide to suck it up and wait them out until they move on, I've found that the subsequent misery is simple not worth it.

Dont Hire Drongos, Galans or a Bull in a china Shop

- **Hire very carefully and listen to your gut instinct as to whether the person will be capable, competent and a good cultural fit.**

- **If you need to address a people issue, do so directly and work with the person to identify potential resolutions that will add value to both the person and the organization.**

- **If no suitable resolution is available, remove the person but do so respectfully so they can retain dignity. In many cases the person is self-aware and recognizes that they are not suited to their role.**

Chapter Five

—————

'Look Out for Your Mates'

*There's a great Australian tradition of mateship,
reinforced during the hardships of the convict
era, the hard work required to survive in the
Australian bush and the comradeship within the
armed services during multiple wars.*

Once you have a team of people on board, it's extremely important to take care of your employees and be fair to all stakeholders
including customers, partners and investors.

There are multiple aspects to this, but I've found the following to be among the most important:

- Set very clear expectations regarding behavior, performance
  and targets;
- Effectively and regularly communicate on how the team
  and individuals are performing as well as the overall status
  and health of the business;

- Build a sense of shared purpose and find opportunities to strengthen team spirit and comradery;
- Look after the individuals who are part of your team – look for opportunities to help them develop and advance in their career;
- Appropriately reward the team (as a collective) and individuals for their achievements and be clear as to why they are receiving the rewards and the impact they are driving;
- Remember to also find small aspects of their performance to praise and if some aspect of a person's performance is lacking, redirect early rather than waiting for it to become a major issue;
- Set very clear boundaries that relate to how the team and individuals will be treated, particularly with respect to people in power positions such as investors, board members and customers.

Of all the above, the last point may be the hardest but maybe the most important. It sometimes involves putting your own position at risk and the people you are protecting may not even be aware of the situation, but I believe it to be critical to ethical leadership.

I faced this situation where a board of directors agreed that we should seek to take a public company private in order to better maximize our ability to build the business for longer term gain than the public stock markets would allow. I was also in favor of this approach as I felt we had a large opportunity that would require investment over a multi-quarter period and would result in significant growth and a much larger company valuation over time.

However, the situation became very tenuous as we discussed the execution of the go-private plan and it became clear that the board wanted to ensure that they, the investors and certain members of the executive team would hold significant stock in the reconstituted company and hence stand to make significant amounts of money once the company relisted or was acquired. The other side to this was they didn't want any other employees to receive shares or options and hence would not receive any additional reward for their work.

To me this was a complete non-starter. If you ask people to take a journey that could last multiple years, you must appropriately reward them for their efforts and the risks they take alongside you – this is the very essence of "mateship". In this case, I was able to block the go-private plan, which subsequently resulted in me having to leave my position and the company. This was very disappointing to me and distressing to my family as we then relocated once more so I could take up a new role with a different company. I'm still not sure if the people who worked with me were aware of the true circumstances regarding my departure, but I could at least feel good about retaining my integrity and doing the right thing for them.

Another situation where this type of behavior arises is at a significant company event such as an acquisition. I had this situation in a startup that was being acquired where I had to stand firm against investors who were trying to exercise the rights associated with preferred shares, which would have meant that regular employees with common shares would not have received any reward for their time, effort and risks during the multiple years of building the initial company. This in fact happened twice due to a circumstance where we initially were acquired in an all-stock transaction and subsequently there was another event when the acquiring company was itself acquired.

In the first situation, even though my personal gain would have been higher if only the preferred shareholders were paid out (I had invested alongside the external shareholders in every round of funding), I went against the investors and fortunately the shareholdings of the co-founders were sufficient to allow us to block the deal. This allowed us to get to an equitable agreement whereby all shareholders including the employees' common shares and stock options were paid out equally.

In the second case, much to my own distaste and the horror of my wife, I agreed to a side letter guaranteeing an external investor that they would make at least as much money out the acquisition if they converted to common shares and shared equally with all other shareholders, as they would if they retained their preferred shareholdings. This meant I had a potential million-dollar personal liability, but I felt the risk was acceptable and, in any event, necessary given the impact it would have on our employees and their families. In the end this transaction worked out very well for everyone involved, including the recalcitrant shareholder.

In addition to looking out for the team and all relevant stakeholders, it's important to realize the team is comprised of individuals who may need special attention at times. This might be to help them understand their alternatives for development or it might be more personal. This approach was brought home to me rather early in my career.

I had just finished the first startup and was in a hard place financially due to lack of payment as that startup collapsed as outlined in Chapter Two. This situation was made worse as in the move to my role at BMC Software, we thought we had sold our house in California and so bought a house in Houston. The

California house sale fell through which meant two mortgages (I learnt from this and made sure I was never in this position again). At the same time, my wife ended up in the hospital due to a potentially life-threatening illness.

In the midst of this, I received a call asking me to visit with the CEO of BMC, Max Watson, who I hadn't met up to that point. Max told me that he had heard a lot about me, that I was doing very well in my new role, and that he also was aware of my personal circumstances. He then proceeded to give me a very unexpected cash bonus, which not only helped tremendously, but ensured my respect and ongoing loyalty to both BMC and Max.

This type of act of compassion is very meaningful to the people involved, but I believe also makes sound business sense in terms of developing morale.

Look out for Your mates

- Treat your people as you would like to be treated — with respect, compassion, good communications and appropriate rewards.

- While you need to take care of all stakeholders including boards, investors, customers and partners, set appropriate boundaries.

- Remember that the people who've joined you in business are dependent on the business for their livelihoods and the wellbeing of their families, and so look out for them as you would your own family.

- Be prepared to stand up for what's right and for your own beliefs and integrity even if there is personal cost in doing so.

Chapter Six

'Don't Have Tickets
on Yourself'

*This refers to someone who is conceited or vain
and is used mostly when someone thinks too
highly of themselves compared to reality.*

While having a healthy ego and being confident in yourself is an asset, particularly when starting a new endeavor or business venture, there is a point at which over-confidence turns negative. We all have flaws and carry baggage, which requires a certain amount of mindfulness and self-awareness to recognize and adjust for as we seek high performance.

Ego-driven behavior can quickly escalate in a team setting if multiple people start to play a game of "one-upping" each other trying to prove that they're the smartest person in the room. This can be exacerbated if there are any galahs or bulls in the team as described in Chapter Four.

The most effective path to reducing this type of behavior that I've experienced is:

- Be humble and an effective path to this is to adopt an attitude of continuous growth and learning – it's hard to be too conceited once you recognize how much you don't know;
- Lead by example and work beside your team members, particularly when the tasks they must perform are not the most pleasant or fun;
- Seek to learn from others, and look for other people with skills, expertise and experience that could be valuable to you;
- Be prepared to do the dirty work even if it's not in your job description and even if others aren't aware that you're doing it;
- If an ego battle starts with teammates or colleagues, don't participate or play their game – it will dissipate over time.

Some of the best examples of humble leadership (sometimes called servant leadership) that I've experienced have been early in my career with Tony Enberg at HP and much later as I was fortunate to witness Satya Nadella's transition to the role of CEO of Microsoft. In both cases, these leaders demonstrated genuine interest in the people they worked with and who worked for them, and each also had a clear thirst to continue learning and growing.

A great lesson for me personally was very early in my career at Wang Computer when I moved from leading customer support and professional services for one of the states in Australia into a new role as a sales rep. I had been supporting the sales team in many deals and thought that I was very smart, and it was my knowledge of our hardware and software that was the key to closing these deals and that the sales reps I supported were basically lazy.

I was wrong! After moving into sales, I had some very lean months as I couldn't close any deals or even really create any prospective sales, and of course most of my salary was commission-based.

Feeling somewhat humbled I went back and spent time with the more experienced sales reps to better understand how they prospected for business, the way they would develop and build relationships with decision makers, and the techniques they would use to overcome objections and move a potential deal smoothly through the sales cycle.

Obviously, I had a lot to learn but I embraced the challenge and the following year I was in the top three sales reps in Australia and met Dr Wang at the international sales achiever celebration.

This was a lesson that stayed with me and has caused me to ask: "What can I learn from this person or this situation?" many times as I progressed through my career.

In the technology arena, a great example of leaders being willing to work alongside team members happens at trade shows. These tend to be very tiring affairs full of large numbers of attendees where "booth duty" is a necessary way of raising awareness and hopefully creating a list of new prospects for sales.

Earlier in my career, this activity was an expected part of my role in marketing and it was always morale boosting when senior leaders visited the booth and encouraged employees but even more so if they were willing to work the booth, engage with prospective customers and demonstrate the products. Leaders who arranged or participated in team social activities after hours at these trade shows were also very appreciated by the team and this helped to make these events much more enjoyable than would have been the case otherwise.

I took this lesson with me and ensured that whenever possible, as a team leader I would participate in booth duty and other activities such as booth setup and tear-down, furniture movement etc.

Sometimes this goes beyond simply participating alongside team members. One example that stands out for me was when myDIALS moved into our first official office. It was an exciting time but also required some heavy work as we purchased used office furniture (from the Professional Bull Riders Association which seemed appropriate given the challenges ahead of us). This meant renting a large U-Haul truck, driving a couple hours each way to pick up the furniture and then moving the furniture into the new office. Our small team at the time all pitched in, but I made sure I spent additional time arranging the furniture after everyone-else had gone home for the day.

Because money was tight, I took on the duties of office cleaner after hours and over the weekend. We started to make sales, raised external funding and hired more people, which meant we had to move into a new, larger office which came complete with cleaning services. I thought we had really come a long way as I no longer had to clean the toilets!

Don't Have Tickets on Yourself

- Ego itself isn't bad but needs to be balanced with humility and self-awareness.

- Be humble, recognize your weaknesses and strive to continually learn and grow as a leader.

- Don't play the game if some colleagues want to demonstrate their superiority – this could well be an over-compensation for some weakness on their part.

Chapter Seven

'Fair Suck of the Sauce Bottle'

There are multiple versions of this –
'fair crack of the whip', 'fair suck of the sav',
'fair suck of the sauce bottle' –
all meaning the same thing, "be reasonable".

There are many business books that describe how to negotiate to get the best deal, or how to get the other side to agree to your demands. I've always believed that the best deal is a fair one that is advantageous to both parties. In its most simple form, this means that both sides need to be reasonable and willing to compromise to ensure the deal works for each party.

When preparing for such a negotiation, there are three criteria that must be clearly understood:

- The optimal deal that provides the most desired outcome and is also reasonable for the other side;

- The parameters that you're willing to compromise on or give up in order to reach a deal;
- The point at which you will walk away from the deal and the associated "BATNA" – best alternative to negotiated agreement.

In any negotiation there is always the human element, and this is likely to lead to emotions and expectations that run high. Knowing how to handle these situations is a large determining factor in achieving a successful outcome. One of the most effective tools you have is the ability to remain silent at appropriate times both to give the other side time to calm down and reflect, and often the time and space to make another move that might weaken their position and solidify your ability to reach agreement.

Remaining silent and not reacting to an outburst or overreach can be very hard, but I've found this to be most effective in multiple negotiations.

When I was CEO of Citect, we had an independent distribution network outside of Australia. While this had served the company well in the early years, it was time to take more direct control of our international operations so that we could accelerate growth and serve larger customers better. In most countries we had a single master distributor and, in some cases, they had been granted (or maybe just taken) Citect as part of their company name – something that caused confusion and potential devaluation of the Citect brand. These distributors were all smaller, family owned businesses that their owners had built over several years.

This is the classic situation where individual aspirations and emotions come into play. What was most curious to me was two very different reactions – one in South Africa, and one in Germany.

In South Africa the local company was on the brink of large success with multiple large contracts with mining companies in final stages of selection. This was a tremendous achievement for the local team, however the mining companies wanted to deal directly with Citect as a vendor, so the local company could not win the deals unless it was acquired by the parent, and similarly Citect could not win the deals without a strong local presence.

This set the scene for a great win-win outcome, but it was also quite emotional for the owners of the local company as the valuation would primarily be based on current value and would not reflect the full value the combination would realize. This led to many long conversations and in many cases my role was simply to be quiet as the principal on the other side vented about his frustrations in not being able to close the large mining company deals by themselves and hence receive full value for the work they had done. The fairest outcome was to structure the deal with an initial payment, and then an earn-out based on successfully closing and delivering the local deals.

Eventually, the local team understood the value and additional potential of this deal and we were able to finalize negotiations and execute the acquisition. This was a great outcome as once this happened and we successfully delivered the first project, multiple other large projects were awarded, and we were successful in selling to other mining companies based on our reputation for fairness and successful delivery. What made this deal even sweeter was the value of the Rand appreciated significantly after the deal, resulting in a much higher return in Australian currency.

When we made the same move in Germany to acquire the master distributor, we found a different situation. In this case, the primary owner of the local company recognized that they had reached a plateau in their ability to grow the company and a different structure was required in order to scale more broadly geographically and to service larger companies. This should have been a straight-forward negotiation once we established an appropriate value, which also should have been relatively easy as there are clear precedents and guidelines for valuing a distribution and services company.

However, once we were in Germany to conclude negotiations, the owner brought along his accountant who had very different ideas on how to value the company than I had (and probably different to anyone else in the industry). I think the difficulty was primarily because the accountant dealt mostly with industrial companies that had real assets and high-margin proprietary products.

Every time we started to engage in a discussion regarding a fair valuation, the accountant would start shaking his head and repeatedly saying "No!" I had my CFO with me and in breaks we started to call the accountant "Dr. No" (you may have noticed that many professional people in Germany have doctorates). We kept calm and continued to explain the rationale as to how we were approaching valuation. We also remained as quiet as possible, as this allowed the owner time to also talk to the accountant.

At one point just as we were breaking for lunch, the owner mentioned that he had arranged a special evening in a local winery to celebrate if we were successful in reaching an agreement. During lunch, I pulled my CFO aside as I felt this indicated the owner was emotionally committed to the deal, and I wanted both my CFO and I to not give any more concessions and to remain as silent as possible through the afternoon. The only time we did speak was to make it clear that the accountant was off-base when he suggested different, unusual methods for valuing the company – a polite version of the Australian saying, "tell him he's dreaming"!

Sure enough, by mid-afternoon the owner had convinced his accountant that the deal and valuation were fair, and we were able to finalize the term sheet and move forward. That evening we had a wonderful experience sharing a meal with the local owner and the head of the winery including touring the cellars and sampling many different wines.

One of the most difficult negotiations for me was when we sold myDIALS. I had to recognize that I also had some significant emotions to deal with, as we had spent around six years building the company and now were faced with the alternative of either raising a large amount of funding to accelerate our growth or being acquired by a larger company that was also raising a very large round of funding. We already had an OEM deal with this company and there were very strong synergies between the products.

I had spent several months meeting with venture capital firms and had a good understanding of the terms under which we could complete an independent round of funding. This was tempting as we could continue to control our destiny and I would continue to run the company as the CEO.

However, I also had to make a complete assessment of the associated risks and consider the potential outcome for employees and investors. After carefully weighing the alternatives, I and the board decided a merger with the larger company would likely lead to a better outcome with less risk and so we entered negotiations to be acquired. This resulted in a very stressful and somewhat frustrating time for me. I had to work hard to ensure we received the best valuation for the company, and I also had to ensure that every employee was taken care of and would have a valuable role in the combined entity as well as a good financial outcome for themselves.

In the middle of the negotiations, we had some bad news from the Australian Government which changed the rules associated with an R&D tax credit program we had been taking advantage of, resulting in a material lowering of the future value we would receive from the program. This of course made the negotiations harder, and lead to some emotional accusations of hiding this situation (unfortunately I can't control any government including Australia's when they decide to make policy changes).

I also had to work hard with our external investors to ensure we would treat our employees fairly with respect to stock options and vesting. This was made more difficult because we would be acquired by a private company in a stock transaction, making it difficult to place a hard cash valuation on the transaction. Fortunately, between the other founder and myself we had retained enough ownership to be able to block any moves by the external investors and so were able to achieve a fair result for everyone.

After several difficult negotiation sessions, including having to bear the brunt of emotional outbursts from both our investors and the executives of the other company, we reached agreement. One phone call was particularly nasty, and I had to simply stay quiet while the other CEO ranted for several minutes. This was however very telling, as I recognized that he must have told his board that the deal was already done and hence he was fully committed, which gave me the confidence to stand firm and in fact to push for additional concessions for our employees.

In the end this was a very good deal for all concerned – every employee received employment with the new company along with retention bonuses, all employee stock options were fully vested with exercise prices and taxes paid as part of the deal, and investors and employees alike were very well rewarded financially when the combined entity exited through a subsequent IPO process and acquisition.

Fair Suck of the Sauce Bottle

- Enter negotiations in the spirit of a win-win outcome that is fair to both parties.

- Understand the range of outcomes you're willing to accept and the point at which it's better to walk away.

- The ability to remain silent as appropriate, particularly when emotions run high, is a very valuable tool.

- Consider all stakeholders as you determine the viability and attractiveness of any deal. In some cases there will be conflicting desires which will have to be carefully balanced.

Chapter Eight

'Do Some Hard Yakka'

*'Hard yakka' means hard work, in many
cases hard physical work. An alternative saying
is 'put in the hard yards'.*

Whatever job you take, sustained success only comes through inspiration and working hard. I'm not going to delve into the debate about work/life balance as I believe that is a very personal and individual choice and I certainly don't begrudge anyone who decides that it is better for them to work less and enjoy life and family more.

In my own career, while I've tried to achieve some balance, be present at those important family events and to actively participate in the lives of family and friends, I know that I didn't really achieve this, and I also realize this has been particularly hard on my family. The demands of any role today have risen as it seems we're never really "offline" and if you operate within a global company this is exacerbated due to different time zones and cultural expectations.

As you move into more senior roles, the need to be available to your team, particularly if they are geographically dispersed, brings the added element of significant travel, much of which is done outside of normal business time to maximize working hours.

I found this as I moved into a manager role at HP and had a team split between Silicon Valley, Sacramento (Roseville), France, Germany and Denmark. In addition to spending time at each location, I was also on the road visiting with customers, partners and press in various parts of the world resulting in around 60% of my time spent away from home. While this was exciting and a great growth opportunity for me, I recognize that it was a difficult time for my family, particularly as my children were young.

This pattern of significant travel continued for me as I moved to BMC Software and into the executive ranks. I lost count of how many countries I visited as, in addition to the regular visits to our Europe and Asia headquarters and subsidiaries, one of my roles was to officiate at the opening of new offices across the globe. One side benefit was attaining permanent status on multiple airlines and million-miler status on two (I'm not totally sure that's a good thing).

One thing I found is that the extensive travel became such a normal part of my life that I didn't always recognize the impact it was having on my family. This was brought to my attention by my son, who is very good at calling me out.

I was with Citect and living in Sydney at the time, and when we were out to dinner, I said it was good not be travelling so much since I had moved back to Australia. To my surprise my son started laughing at me. This obviously caused me to think, and upon reflection I realized I had been taking a "round the world trip" for a couple weeks every quarter to review our operations and in the meantime making side trips to various locations in Australia and Asia. It surprised me just how much I was out of touch with the reality of my situation.

I tried to take advantage of some of my international travel by tacking on some personal time and whenever possible flying my family in to join me on a vacation. This worked out well with my wife, son and daughter participating in trips to the UK, Germany, Italy, Spain and China – all of which were educational as well as fun times. I'd encourage anyone who travels a lot for work to look for opportunities to include your family when possible. It can also be a good idea to take some time for yourself – it's amazing how much you can see and experience in a day if you have a personal guide. I took advantage of some downtime in Budapest and in Israel by hiring a personal guide and driver in each location, which made for very interesting and educational visits.

It always seemed that no matter which company I was with, the hours were long and extended into the weekends. Earlier in my career I wasn't good at separating work from weekend family time and I know this caused some stress and impacted my relationships. As I progressed in my career, I started to shut down and go offline on the weekends – at least from Friday evening to Sunday midday. This was much healthier and still allowed time on Sunday afternoon and evening to prepare for the coming week.

While successfully pursuing a career at large companies is demanding, (Microsoft was probably the highlight for this), working in a startup brings the long hours and much more. It feels like there is so much more at stake and I believe that this is generally the case. In both of my first two startups I worked the long hours, travelled extensively and had the dubious joy of working without pay for many months.

At my first startup, I was very excited to be an executive and company officer for the first time and took an apartment in Los Angeles away from my family and even bought my first Mercedes as I was sure it was going to be a very interesting and rewarding move. Well, it was interesting. As outlined in Chapter Two, the company was sued for trade secret violation, which certainly introduced me to the downsides of the American legal system, gave me an ongoing distrust and distaste for most lawyers, and led to a period of tremendous uncertainty and difficulty.

While the initial intent was that I would work in Los Angeles for 3-4 days a week and spend the rest of the time working from home, as the company cash situation deteriorated due to the cost of the lawsuit, I couldn't travel home as much and tended to spend several weeks in LA or on the road visiting prospective customers, partners and investors. This caused additional stress for the family and after we placed the company into Chapter 7 bankruptcy, our personal finances were in a mess, so I had to find a new job quickly to pay outstanding bills and the Mercedes was rapidly sold.

I was also in the position of not taking a salary when I co-founded myDIALS, but at least my finances were in a very different position and it was a deliberate decision. In this case the stress wasn't as much about whether I would be hurt financially (although I had a significant percentage of my net worth invested in the company over multiple funding rounds), but more about the financial well-being of the employees who had joined the company. As with many startups we had a couple of occasions where it was doubtful how much longer we could make payroll, but in each case we were able to find the next large customer win, the next partnership or the next round of investment.

It is a great motivator when you think about the families of the employees who have trusted you and who could be earning larger salaries at other companies – it really makes the hard work involved with a startup worthwhile.

Do Some Hard Yakka

- Set expectations with family and friends and ensure that both you and they are prepared for the downsides of aggressively pursuing strong career growth.

- Look for opportunities to include your family in unique opprtunities wherever possible – such as travel or experiences made possible by your work situation.

- Take time for yourself, particularly when you have some downtime in a foreign location. I've found long plane flights to be a great time for thinking and reflection, and attending conferences as a participant can also provide new insights and perspectives.

- Understand that startups bring their own set of challenges (and rewards) and set your own expectations realistically.

Chapter Nine

'Hit the Frog and Toad'

'Frog and toad' is rhyming slang for "road" –
hence this saying means "hit the road",
sometimes used to tell someone to get lost,
but in this case, we'll use it as getting out on
the road to meet real people in the real world.

While centralized planning and decision making has its place in the life of a professional, there is really nothing more insightful than meeting directly with a variety of employees, customers, prospective customers, industry analysts and influencers, partners and other business professionals and stakeholders. I've found this to be true in every role I've had, and this becomes much more important when you have a distributed company, particularly if it operates in more than one country.

Cultural differences and different ways of conducting business in different countries mean central decisions can be sub-optimal or lead to disaster. Of course, there is also the counterbalance, where it can be easy for the local management team to claim that everything coming from corporate headquarters is wrong and they must do everything differently, even if this is not the case.

I've been fortunate to travel extensively for business and I've lost count of the number of countries I've visited and where I've had business meetings or conducted business. In each case, I've learnt a lot and it has helped to shape my ideas and approach to business and dealing with others.

My first business trip abroad was to the USA in the early 1980s and the energy, enthusiasm and can-do attitude I found in Silicon Valley was truly inspiring. It seemed as though nothing was impossible in the world of software, chips and computer design, even though this was long before cellular networks, mobile phones, pervasive personal computing and the internet. This trip also introduced me to the concept of "work hard, play hard", which I must admit made a lot of sense to a young Aussie lad at the time.

Since that first trip I've spent considerable time in a business context in various countries in Europe and Asia as well as time in South Africa and Israel. Here are some high-level observations and learnings I've taken away from those trips:

- Business in Europe tends to be more relationship-based than business in the USA. Time must be spent establishing rapport and assessing the willingness of the other party to deal fairly within the construct of a long-term relationship versus a simple one-time business transaction. This will require some time spent away from the office building a personal relationship for large deals and important ongoing partnerships.
- For the most part, doing business in Asian countries is even more dependent on building relationships and it

may take multiple meetings just establishing credibility and building rapport before the business subject can even be broached. I found this to be particularly the case in Japan where it was important not only to establish credibility up-front, but also to reinforce commitment to successfully delivering the required result at a final meeting, before any deal could be consummated. As the CEO of Citect, I took several trips to Japan to personally commit our company resources to ensuring a successful project before we could finalize a contract.

- Business operations in some countries tends to be very consensus-driven, which I found to be the case in the Nordics. Here, time must be spent educating and getting the buy-in of multiple different influencers in addition to the ultimate decision makers.

- In other countries, the business may be very hierarchical which can bring its own challenges, particularly when dealing with a local office or subsidiary. I found this to be the case in China. When I would travel to China to inspect the performance of our subsidiary there, I had to take extra precautions to ensure I was getting the real situation and not just what the leader wanted portrayed. I would meet individually with mid-level managers and assure them that there would be no repercussions no matter what they divulged. I also came to understand and then knew to ask for the various versions of the company accounts. There could be three versions – one that was used by local management, one that was for local authorities and one for corporate headquarters. These were all slightly different and each presented a different perspective, and so the combination was required to understand the full picture.

- I also learnt about different labor laws and came to understand that operations had to be modified to align with these. On one of my first trips to Germany we wanted to do some work outside business hours and in order to go into the office during a national holiday, special dispensation had to be sought from local authorities. I found out more about local labor laws when we had to fire employees in France and the UK. This is certainly more difficult than in the USA with its at-will employment.

- In Israel I learnt to be patient with negotiations, to use silence and to be prepared to walk away if the deal wasn't fair or was taking so much time and energy that it was distracting the rest of the business. It seemed the Israelis were willing to continue negotiating indefinitely and being able to walk away (and not be bluffing) was an important aspect of closing the negotiation.

Sometimes there are unusual or difficult reasons to visit a local office. I once discovered an unusual order pattern in one of our subsidiaries where we primarily sold through a distribution channel. Orders would be placed just prior to the end of a fiscal quarter and then either cancelled or modified early in the new fiscal quarter. This was something I couldn't clarify with international phone calls (this was before widespread use of video conferencing which may have helped, but I still think wouldn't have been as effective as meeting in person).

So, without telling anyone in the local subsidiary I flew in and visited a number of the distribution partners who came clean that they were placing orders to help the local management team achieve quarterly performance goals with the understanding they could cancel or modify them after the quarter had closed.

This behavior is fraudulent and resulted in the removal of the local leader and the head of finance as well as a severe reprimand for the local sales management. It also resulted in a very awkward meeting with our auditors.

I've also found it very beneficial to meet personally with other business professionals, industry figures and influencers. In each case, taking the time to get to know these people has led to additional insights that would not have been possible in the more impersonal world of email, phone calls and social media. Similarly, just spending time with employees can be extremely beneficial in identifying high-potential talent, issues with management practices and opportunities to increase effectiveness and efficiency.

This can be very important when either taking on a new role that includes a new team reporting to you, or even more so when acquiring a company, which comes with its own culture and set of operating norms. One of the responsibilities I had as head of corporate strategy at BMC Software was to act as the transition manager for newly acquired companies. Small actions can mean a lot to employee morale as there is usually an amount of uncertainty after an acquisition.

I spent several weeks in Boston after one acquisition and it became apparent that there was some angst over the senior leaders having assigned parking spaces close to the building entrance while everyone-else had to walk further, sometimes through snow. Assigned parking was not a practice at corporate headquarters and so we eliminated parking assignments and I was surprised as how well that was received across the new team.

Alternatively, corporate edicts can be detrimental and have unintended consequences. During this time, BMC had a strict no-smoker policy for employees, I think because our health benefits were self-funded. This worked okay while we were hiring employees at the corporate headquarters, but we inherited several smokers with an acquisition we made in California.

Again, I was temporarily located to the new subsidiary to manage the transition. While we offered smoking cessation programs it became clear to me this was not a real solution, particularly after the building was nearly set on fire by smokers hiding in the bushes behind the building so they could smoke unseen.

A call that started with "Houston, we have a problem" resulted in changes to our employee policy regarding smoking.

Getting out of the office, meeting people, seeing what's really happening across the company, partners, competitors and your industry can be extremely enlightening and is one of most important tools for any manager or business leader.

Hit the Frog and Toad

- Look for opportunities to experience business in different locations and cultures – thiss will broaden your perspective and enable you to be holistic in your thinking.

- Sometimes the only way to get to the truth is to spend time with individuals both formally and outside the office.

- Spend time with a variety of people – employees, partners, industry influencers, and other professionals as this can broaden your perspective significantly.

Chapter Ten

'Give Mate's Rates'

*As the term 'mate's rates' suggests, this refers
to a level of discount or special service usually
only given to friends of the person or company
selling the product or service.*

Once you have defined and begun development of the product
or service, it's time to start recruiting advisors, early adopters and
influencers who can help refine the offering and contribute to
early success. Attracting the right set of people who can evaluate
and hopefully validate your offering is a key element of achieving
product market fit. While for the initial set of prospects you may
need to provide the service either free or at cost, I believe you do
need to charge a viable amount for most early customers in order
to validate market acceptance of the value equation.

Even with this proviso, you can be quite creative when
it comes to structuring these early deals. If it's a subscription
service, offering an elongated or discounted initial period that

then changes to regular price on renewal or over several renewals can be an effective way of both incentivizing early customers and validating the price point. Other alternatives are to bundle the offering with other products or services already being consumed, or to offer free or heavily discounted implementation services.

My first experience with this approach was at HP when we developed a new offering, PerfView as described in Chapter One. Because this was a new category of product, gaining early adopters was very important to validate the need and the approach we were taking. We also wanted to drive new sales and revenue to boost the business unit performance for that fiscal year, and hence we needed not only evaluators but early paying customers.

We structured a multi-tier program:

- Early adopters to evaluate initial prototypes and provide feedback and guidance;
- Beta customers who would receive very favorable pricing and terms in return for formally testing the product and then providing testimonials;
- A larger group of trial customers who would receive early access to the product but convert to paying customers immediately we formally released the product as Generally Available.

This approach was very successful in guiding the direction and functionality of the offering, ensuring a quality product and helping to achieve a great financial result for the year.

One of the best examples of convincing prospective customers to sign on early was when I was at Citect and we developed the new Manufacturing Execution System – Citect Ampla (also described in Chapter One). In this case, the head of the new unit, Peter Long, was a master at both describing the offering and benefits and also very adept at using PowerPoint and other tools to show very realistic mock-ups of the product interface and outcomes.

I was always amazed when customers' eyes would light up at the possibility of our planned product and Peter was able to convince multiple customers to sign up as paying customers on the proviso that we delivered the product to match the specifications we had outlined. There were two incentives for these customers – early access to a product that solved a very real problem for them, and we offered free implementation and training services to ensure they received rapid value.

Also helpful for determining product direction and validating offerings are customer councils and advisory boards. These can take many shapes although I've found some characteristics to be important to the value these provide:

- Ensure participants are in the target market demographic and representative of the prospective customer size, industry, geography and maturity;
- Within this constraint, ensure the people are as diverse as possible and willing to voice their opinions in a constructive manner;
- Members of an advisory board or a customer council can also be valuable in providing testimonials to analysts and press and in influencing other prospective customers to evaluate your offering. To be most valuable, these people should be known within the industry or their companies should be recognizable, and they should be current, active and respected.

We formed an advisory board during the early days of myDIALS, almost as soon as we had begun the initial product development. This was a diverse set of individuals who brought multiple perspectives to the table – in addition to a CIO at a large target company, we included a respected executive at a leading management consulting firm to contribute to our strategy, a former HR executive at multiple large companies provided input on people practices, a CFO of multiple public and private companies provided financial guidance, a former CEO of a large public company offered general business and management advice and an industry analyst brought both technical and market insight.

I truly appreciated the input and guidance provided by all these members and they provided strong support and reassurance even when we went through some difficult times.

These board members should be recognized for their time and expertise and the most appropriate form is through stock options which aligns their rewards with the company success. I found this to be helpful but also respected members who chose not to accept these as there could be a perceived conflict if they became customers – which is an even better outcome. Several of the board members also invested directly in myDIALS alongside other external investors in one or more of our funding rounds – again a great outcome and clearly a vote of confidence in the company and what we were doing.

There are firms that specialize in helping with recruiting members for advisory boards and these can be helpful if your contact base is limited, however I don't believe this can be fully outsourced. I experienced this at another company where a third party recruited and managed the advisory board which I then inherited when I joined as an executive.

I found that while the members were willing to offer their thoughts and guidance, they were not all relevant and up to date on the market as several had retired some years earlier, and it was very difficult to get other members to engage with press, analysts or other prospective customers.

In hindsight, the company should have taken more responsibility in the recruitment, vetting and clearly setting expectations of these board members.

Give mates' Rates

- Sign up early adopters and advisory board members who can provide early guidance, validate company direction, help refine products to ensure product/market fit and help avoid costly mistakes.

- Provide appropriate incentives that align outcomes for the board members and the company.

- Actively manage these early adopters and boards to gain maximum value for both the company and the participants.

Chapter Eleven

'No Worries Mate, She'll Be Right'

'No worries' seems to have become much more popular worldwide (maybe due to Crocodile Dundee), but 'no worries' and 'she'll be right' combine to express the belief that "whatever is wrong now will right itself with time".

When building a business or pursuing a career path, there will be times when it feels like the weight of the world is on your shoulders and nothing is going right. These can be tough times – I've experienced several. However, although the path to success is never really a straight line, I've found that provided you persevere, the immediate struggles will resolve themselves and, in many cases, lead to a better outcome than you might think possible at the time.

There is a saying I've used often – "this too shall pass", which apparently comes from an Eastern monarch a long time ago. More recently the sentiment that "Everything will all be alright in the end, and if it's not alright, it's not yet the end" from the movie The Best Exotic Marigold Hotel, also sums up this sentiment.

I experienced a very ironic twist with my first startup which went into Chapter 7 Bankruptcy due to a lawsuit from a much larger company, as described in Chapter Two. The CEO of the startup and the CEO of the suing company had worked together previously at BMC Software, so obviously there were some outstanding issues, which I wasn't aware of when I joined the startup. However, the twist came when I needed a job and was recruited by BMC Software in a product marketing role, which then led to a very successful time in my career.

There will most likely be many times of crisis or despair if you go down the path of building a startup, and I experienced a number of these at myDIALS. The first of these came following the initial seed funding and after the first external fund raising from people I knew personally and who were connected with the company in some way. We had developed the product and had the initial customers but needed a larger round of funding to continue building out the product as well as a sales team.

This proved difficult with traditional venture capital as we were very early into using the cloud-based Software as a Service model for business intelligence, and there was a good deal of skepticism that businesses would be willing to trust a startup with the security of their critical business data. This was also when the financial markets were collapsing during the Global Financial Crisis. We were getting very close to running out of cash and of course the thought of not being able to make payroll was very troubling.

I was very fortunate to meet Natasha Biegert at an industry event. Her father had made a significant amount of money, primarily in the cattle and meat processing industries, and they had set up a family fund to diversify their holdings, which Natasha was managing. I met with Natasha and Scott Whitefoot, who was the administrator of the fund, multiple times over the course of a few days and they were intrigued by our business model. So, it was time to meet the principal, Jeff Biegert, to see if we could reach an agreement for the fund raise.

This was an interesting meeting that was scheduled for an hour or two but ended up lasting most of the day. It also started with Jeff saying he didn't like technology and that he only made investments when he got a majority ownership. We spent the day exploring the technology, doing demonstrations, delving into the early customer case studies and working through the business model and plan. By the end of the day, we had a deal where the Biegert family would take a minority position under very fair terms and a good valuation. In a matter of a week we had the cash in the bank and could continue to grow the business.

While we had good runway and there was a subsequent external fund raise, again led by the Biegert family, we were still burning cash and were once again in jeopardy of running out of cash a few years later. In this case, we were in the process of evolving our go-to-market model to be more channel-focused as outlined in Chapter Three. While the business potential with the new resale model with NetSuite was strong, it would take some time to develop the partnership, alter the product to enable a "white-label" branding, and train the partner sales and support staff before we would see revenue.

Of course, this wouldn't help our looming cash crisis. I was already working on an OEM deal with Adaptive Planning, and so I set about negotiating up-front royalties against future sales in order to alleviate our immediate situation. I'm very grateful to John Peters (acting CEO of Adaptive at the time) and Rob Hull (the company founder) as they agreed to the upfront royalties in exchange for some additional favorable terms for them.

Our relationship with Adaptive Planning was to take another turn several months later. While the OEM agreement had bought us time, and the resale agreement with NetSuite (a public software company) was starting to produce results, we still needed additional funding if we were to realize the full opportunity in front of us.

So once more I began the many meetings with venture capital firms in Silicon Valley and in the Boston area. Once again, I found the VC firms were difficult to deal with as they preferred companies located closer to them, and the terms many suggested didn't seem (at least to me) to recognize the full value we had already created.

Interestingly, Adaptive Planning was also out seeking a major fundraise at the same time. The VC firm that became most interested in investing in myDIALS was also moving towards an investment in Adaptive Planning. They recognized the product synergies already demonstrated through the OEM agreement and so suggested their preferred path was for myDIALS to be acquired by Adaptive Planning as a step in the funding.

While it was frustrating that we wouldn't continue as a stand-alone entity and I had put much effort into the fund raising (and flew many miles from one coast to the other), on balance this was the right decision and it led to a very good financial outcome for all stakeholders including our employees.

No Worries, She'll be Right

- Accept that tough times will arise in any endeavor that includes an amount of risk – whether building a business or making career decisions.

- Remain optimistic, even though business life, particularly in a startup, can feel like a roller-coaster, and seek alternative answers to each dilemma as this will generally lead to a better outcome.

- Be persistent and persevere as it may take some time before you experience the value or goodness that can come from adversity.

Epilogue/Conclusion

Having a successful, fulfilling career is mostly about taking calculated risks, being prepared to work hard and taking a common-sense approach to business. The most important aspect of most businesses (particularly in technology) is the people who provide the inspiration, expertise and perspiration to deliver valuable offerings and achieve business success.

Understanding the importance of people, it makes sense to hire the right people taking into consideration their skills, work ethic, interpersonal relationships and cultural fit. Once you have the right people on board, treat them with respect, nurture them and their career aspirations, and reward them well for taking the journey with you.

There will likely be many times in your career when things are not going the way you'd prefer, when working life becomes a hard slog and not much fun. It's important to maintain a positive attitude, summon your inner optimism, and persevere. It is highly likely that there are better times ahead and the trying times strengthen and develop you both as a person and a professional.

All the best to you in your career and remember that it will all be good in the end – no worries mate!

Acknowledgements

Thank you to the people who have most influenced me throughout my career. My earliest mentors were Bill Allard at Wang and Tony Engberg at HP who both demonstrated effective leadership. Max Watson, Bill Austin and Roy Wilson, the former CEO, CFO and HR head respectively of BMC Software all provided support, advice and guidance both at BMC and subsequently as I continued my career. Similarly, Dianne Ledingham of Bain & Company has been a work partner, advisor, investor and friend.

I experienced multiple leadership styles at Microsoft, some great, some terrible, but the most inspiring was the true leadership demonstrated by Satya Nadella.

I've had the pleasure of working with multiple people more than once in my career including Kirill Tatarinov, Neil Holloway, Pam Austin and Karri Alexion-Tiernan who I worked with at Microsoft and elsewhere, and who inspired me with their vision and work ethic. I also had the pleasure of working with multiple people both at Citect and myDIALS.

I particularly appreciate my co-founder of myDIALS, Peter Long, whose vision, work ethic, integrity and friendship mean so much to me. I am humbled by the early recruits who joined myDIALS when we were starting from nowhere to build a business, including Tim Berston, Tony Watkins, Tim Munro, Luan Lam, Andrew Allan, Kane Fasham and Jeff Balentine. Without your vision, effort, perseverance and early investment it would never have got off the ground.

I also want to thank the members of myDIALS' advisory board and the external investors of myDIALS who contributed the funding necessary to build a viable product, attract customers and partners and achieve a valuable exit including Max Watson, Bill Austin, Roy Wilson, Dianne Ledingham, Jeff Biegert, Natasha Harris, Scott Whitefoot, Michael Lomman, Darren Trumeter, Susan Aldrich, Owen Bobeldyk, John Graff and Peter Pitsker.

Finally, I've enjoyed working with and learnt much from my colleagues at Skytap including Thor Culverhouse, Frank Colich, Brad Schick, Jon Schrader and Jill Domanico.

About the Author

A proven entrepreneur, Wayne Morris has more than 30 years of experience in executive management, strategy, marketing, sales and technical roles in software, services and hardware companies.

Most recently he was Skytap's Chief Marketing Officer, where he led all aspects of marketing including corporate, digital, field and partner marketing. He was instrumental in positioning the company and its products as a leader in the cloud market focused on the large opportunity for migrating traditional applications to the cloud and then modernizing the infrastructure, development processes and architecture of those applications.

Prior to Skytap, Morris was the Corporate Vice President of Microsoft Business Solutions (MBS) marketing at Microsoft Corp, where he helped to elevate the CRM and ERP offerings and significantly increase revenues.

Before joining Microsoft, Morris co-founded and was CEO and a board member of myDIALS, a SaaS start-up that delivers business intelligence providing real-time insight directly to operational decision makers, where he created the company vision, formed successful partnerships with other software companies and successfully negotiated the acquisition of the company by

Adaptive Insights, a complementary SaaS vendor to ensure higher growth.

Previously, Morris was Senior Vice President, worldwide marketing at McData Corporation, a storage area network vendor, where he drove major acquisition integration as well as channel expansion and increased marketing effectiveness. Morris has also held executive leadership positions at global organizations such as Citect Corporation (ASX), BMC Software, Enterprise Software Corp. and HP.

Morris is co-author of "Foundations of Service Level Management," published by SAMS. He has a Bachelor of Science with a major in Computer Science from University of Queensland, Australia.

Morris has taken a "gap year" to travel to a variety of locations across the globe before he and his wife move to a waterfront property in Hawaii.